IT'S TIME TO EAT GRAHAM CRACKERS

It's Time to Eat GRAHAM CRACKERS

Walter the Educator

Silent King Books
A WhichHead Entertainment Imprint

Copyright © 2024 by Walter the Educator

All rights reserved. No part of this book may be reproduced in any manner whatsoever without written per- mission except in the case of brief quotations embodied in critical articles and reviews.

First Printing, 2024

Disclaimer

This book is a literary work; the story is not about specific persons, locations, situations, and/or circumstances unless mentioned in a historical context. Any resemblance to real persons, locations, situations, and/or circumstances is coincidental. This book is for entertainment and informational purposes only. The author and publisher offer this information without warranties expressed or implied. No matter the grounds, neither the author nor the publisher will be accountable for any losses, injuries, or other damages caused by the reader's use of this book. The use of this book acknowledges an understanding and acceptance of this disclaimer.

It's Time to Eat GRAHAM CRACKERS is a collectible early learning book by Walter the Educator suitable for all ages belonging to Walter the Educator's Time to Eat Book Series. Collect more books at WaltertheEducator.com

USE THE EXTRA SPACE TO TAKE NOTES AND DOCUMENT YOUR MEMORIES

GRAHAM CRACKERS

The clock says it's snack time, hooray, let's cheer!

It's Time to Eat

Graham Crackers

A crunchy delight is finally here.

Golden and sweet, with a cinnamon trace,

Graham crackers bring smiles to every face.

Line them up neatly, one, two, and three,

Break them apart, it's so fun to see!

Snap goes the sound as they split with a crack,

Ready to nibble, time for a snack!

Plain or with honey, they're tasty and neat,

They're crispy and light, the perfect treat.

Pair them with milk, so creamy and cold,

Snack time's a treasure, worth more than gold!

Spread peanut butter, or jelly on top,

A graham cracker sandwich will make you stop.

Bananas or chocolate, marshmallows too,

So many toppings, what will you do?

It's Time to Eat

Graham Crackers

Take a big bite and feel the crunch,

Graham crackers are perfect for any munch.

At picnics, at home, or while on the go,

Their yummy goodness steals the show!

Build a small house, stack them up high,

Graham crackers turn builders—oh my, oh my!

Make tiny walls and a roof so sweet,

Then eat it all up, what a fun feat!

Dip them in pudding or yogurt so creamy,

Graham crackers make everything dreamy.

No forks, no spoons, just fingers will do,

A snack full of fun for me and for you!

On rainy days or in sunshine so bright,

Graham crackers make every snack time just right.

Pack them in bags or on picnic plates,

It's Time to Eat

Graham Crackers

Their flavor is magic, their crunch so great.

Share with a friend, because snacks taste best,

When laughter and crackers make hearts feel blessed.

A piece for you and a piece for me,

Sharing is love, as sweet as can be.

So here's to graham crackers, a snack-time star,

No matter where you are, near or far.

Enjoy every crunch, each bite is a treat,

It's Time to Eat

Graham Crackers

Snack time with crackers is always so sweet!

ABOUT THE CREATOR

Walter the Educator is one of the pseudonyms for Walter Anderson. Formally educated in Chemistry, Business, and Education, he is an educator, an author, a diverse entrepreneur, and he is the son of a disabled war veteran. "Walter the Educator" shares his time between educating and creating. He holds interests and owns several creative projects that entertain, enlighten, enhance, and educate, hoping to inspire and motivate you. Follow, find new works, and stay up to date with Walter the Educator™

at WaltertheEducator.com

www.ingramcontent.com/pod-product-compliance
Lightning Source LLC
LaVergne TN
LVHW010623070526
838199LV00063BA/5249